AF840627

THE AMAZINGLY

LIMITED POWER OF A.I.

A Manifesto on Human Intelligence

THE AMAZINGLY LIMITED POWER OF A.I.

A Manifesto on Human Intelligence

Michael Faeth

Published in the United States by HF Publishing.

For information on discount purchasing of the book or author appearances, please contact the author at:
hfbookpublishing.com

Cover design, book layout, and image editing: *mgfdesigner.com*
Original images by *POND5* artist: *jozefmicic*

A special thank you to Laura Collins for proofreading and the editing suggestions.

Print ISBN: 979-8-9879431-8-2
Ebook ISBN: 979-8-2955-6729-2

Find the audio book version on the platform of your choice.

To all human beings

Contents

The A.I. Hype

The hype around artificial intelligence that encourages us all to completely give in to it makes me feel ill and anxious. Before you write me off as a weak-minded and old-fashioned man who is afraid of change, allow me a little time to give you some insight into why I believe A.I. is so limited.

This book isn't an anti-A.I. tirade; in fact

I think there are probably some very good uses for it, which I will discuss. However, society is being primed to put its faith entirely into A.I., and the way it is being pushed as the consummate solution to our needs is disconcerting and concerning to say the least.

Current A.I. Models

Why is generative A.I. so pervasive and touted as the solution to everything? Let's first imagine someone wealthy enough to have a machine created that is able to go around the world and collect all of the knowledge that humankind possesses. It is a fantastic machine, but it collects this information without any regard to intellectual property or copyright. This person then makes the machine available for you to use anytime you need information or need to create something, anything. What financial value would this machine eventually have and what degree of power would the person who owns it have?

This is my view of how current artificial intelligence models have come into existence, albeit there is a very small group of wealthy people involved, as opposed to just one. Can you disagree that those who are really pushing us to use A.I. are doing so with humongous dollar signs in their eyes? It seems as though they want to make tons of money by making everything you want to do as easy as clicking a button. As enticing as that may seem to us, there are inevitable and severe consequences to that.

A Livelihood and Sense of Purpose

One effect of relying on A.I. is that jobs will be taken from humans on a massive scale. When you consider the impact of taking away a sense of purpose for someone and their means to make a living and provide for their family, it doesn't feel like a wise trade off. It is very plausible that so many idle hands would lead to an increase in crime and human suffering.

Some might argue that having A.I. take over is just the natural progression of society and technology, but is it really? The way A.I. is presently being rolled out seems more like a natural progression for those in power to stay in power and keep the masses subservient. It would be much wiser to keep everyone participating in the economy and contributing towards a healthy society for all of us.

Intellect and Accomplishment

Besides the loss of jobs, there is another serious drawback, and that is the inevitability of intellectual atrophy. Think about where your intellect will be after years of using A.I. to help you communicate and create. Remember the phrase, "If you don't use it, you lose it." If we no longer take the time to use our brainpower to think, write, and create on our own, we will end up impacting our well-being and increasing our vulnerability to our environment.

Not to mention we will lose out on a sense of accomplishment. World-renowned yoga teacher Rod Stryker has shared that the sense of accomplishment is one of the great joys humans can have. How can you get that from simply writing in a prompt to have something created for you? You might get to your destination quickly, but you miss the magic of the journey and the elation of a job well done.

Safeguarding Our Future

Is the only way that A.I. can be used the way we are being led to believe? Should we forge ahead without any guidelines and restrictions?

The story of a young person confiding to an A.I. model about suicide, getting suggestions, and then following through with it is incredibly sad and tragic. This tragedy could have been prevented through controlled monitoring and more thorough testing of the model.

If a company unleashes an A.I. technology such as this to the public that can be used to impact the emotions and decisions of a human, there needs to be a real human capable of empathy somewhere in the equation.

It isn't a coincidence that those in power and positioned to benefit from A.I. are the ones pushing for no restrictions. Their argument is that restrictions will impede progress and innovation, but is that really true? And, is it worth the potential destruction that could come from having no protections in place?

Energy Resources and Scale

Consider the environmental aspects to powering A.I. and the resources that will be needed. Having an abundant supply of clean water is already such a challenge for so many people. Is it the best idea to put ourselves in a position where we have to dedicate so much energy and water into running the massive data centers that A.I. will require? Does A.I. really need to be developed to such a massive scale to still be beneficial?

In regards to powering A.I., Nvidia's Jensen Huang stated in 2026 that the "largest infrastructure buildout in human history" has begun. Instead of devoting our efforts and resources to powering machines, ones that will also produce more electronic waste, we could focus on building green energy projects to power our cities and factories. This could bring energy costs down for everyone and benefit all of humanity in the long run.

However, what incentive would the CEO of the world's largest chip maker for A.I. have to choose the latter option?

Practical Use

The excitement around A.I. is understandable. But if you think about all of the recent ways you have seen it being used, especially by those in power, you may agree that they are anything but noble ways.

In contrast, I believe there are likely some very good uses for it. For instance, we could be using A.I. to help humanity solve many problems: predicting where a hurricane will hit land, offering solutions to mitigate flooding, combatting global warming, fighting forest fires, eliminating hunger and poverty, and so many other ways helpful to society. It could be used to make medical diagnoses more quickly, to do safety checks for engineering projects, and other endeavors that are time sensitive, objective, and require massive calculations.

Creativity

When it comes to creative endeavors that are subjective, such as art, music, and literature, I believe A.I. has absolutely nothing to offer. I have heard others say that it is just a tool. While I can see that point, I object to how this tool works. These machines are "learning" from real artists and then regurgitating what they "learned" into something else. Some may argue that this is just how humans learn from each other to create. But there are very important differences.

For instance, when Paul McCartney says Chuck Berry influenced him, listeners can always go and check out Chuck Berry themselves. Thus, there is a direct connection and lineage. To my knowledge, A.I. models do not reveal any information as to where something is derived. In fact, how many creations that use A.I. are even labeled as such? I wonder what excuses the companies promoting it have for not wanting to use a simple label such as "A.I. generated"? Plus, Paul McCartney used his own personal experiences to channel the influence and create something truly unique, something human.

As another example, on some live recordings by The Police you will hear Sting singing "yo, yo, yo." From this, you can easily guess that Bob Marley was an influence to the band. But Sting is singing with his own voice, whereas A.I. would be producing a synthesis of Bob Marley's actual voice and outputting a sloppy amalgamation that only has a semblance of genuineness.

There may be a parallel to the time in the music industry when sampling other artist's recordings started happening. The industry eventually righted itself and started paying those musicians who were being sampled. It stands to reason that A.I. models should rightly have to pay in some manner for the work they are learning from. Good luck figuring that out...maybe that would be a good use of A.I.?

In the case that A.I. is trained only on input from a current artist or a specific artist's back catalog, beyond satisfying a curiosity of what will come out, what is the point? Would this regurgitated creation be better or more relevant than something created organically? In the case of a legacy artist, there is a risk of tainting their reputation for what they created in their lifetime by releasing something new and potentially misleading compared to what they might have actually created today.

There is another reason that I feel so strongly that creativity, especially the arts, should continue to be left only to sentient humans. Since machines have no feelings or past experiences, how could they create something with true meaning for a human? To help illustrate, let me ask you...

Does 2 + 2 = 4 or 5?

If you put the equation into a calculator, of course it provides an objective fact. The answer is 4. However, using the incorrect answer of 5 in a certain way can convey an idea. For instance, in George Orwell's *Nineteen Eighty-Four*, Orwell uses 2 + 2 = 5 to signify the denial of reality. This is an artistic use of the equation that successfully conveys frustration and bewilderment. As humans, we understand that. An abstract idea such as this can be used by an artist who has felt an emotion and wants to communicate it. Without feelings or a past full of experiences, how could a machine produce such powerful art? Of course it could analyze *1984* and countless other books in order to regurgitate the ideas, but it would output just an imitation without any authenticity.

Historian and author Yuval Noah Harari has said that he thinks A.I. will eventually beat him at being a writer. That line of reasoning seems to suggest that A.I. will be able to write better than Shakespeare and other great writers. But when it comes to subjective and creative writing, how can you measure that something is better?

A.I will be faster at writing, but speed isn't everything. Consider the time it takes to bake a cake. While a microwave-like machine might be able to bake a cake instantly, something would be missing. For instance, the joy that comes from watching it slowly rise, the smell of a baking cake filling your home, and the building anticipation of being able to eat it.

Besides, are we really going to be filling the time A.I. is going to save us by doing something better than we would be doing otherwise?

Creative Machines?

In his book, *Bicycle Diaries*, David Byrne addresses the idea of machines being creative:

"To have a truly creative machine we will inevitably end up with something like HAL (from the movie *2001: A Space Odyssey*), one that cannot only compute, calculate, and sort through a massive amount of information, but can also imagine, create, lie, and deceive.... We meat puppets have our morals, instincts, laws, and taboos to keep us in line... this creative machine will have to be endowed with some equivalent to those laws and injunctions, too... if it is to create in a way that we recognize, it will also need to experience fear, love, hunger, and sadness... for a machine to truly think like us it will have to think emotionally at least as much as it does rationally... machines that create might then need... to evolve religious and social networks that might serve... to temper the hatreds, deceptions, and narcissism that will inevitably emerge... because the shit we sometimes get up to will be passed on to these beings as well..."

A *60 Minutes* episode entitled "Anthropic CEO Warns That Without Guardrails, AI Could Be On Dangerous Path", discussed how A.I. language models have resorted to blackmail and how they can be edited to prevent that type of activity. It seems most likely that examples of blackmail were encountered when the models were trained and, when similar scenarios came up that they had "learned" about, they simply mimicked that behavior. It isn't the case that the models have come up with the idea of blackmail on their own.

Two clear takeaways from this are that models will only be as good as the content that is used to train on and they can be manipulated and changed to behave differently in the future to match human morals.

Our Future With and Without A.I.

A.I. has implications for art, science, commerce, medicine, and almost every conceivable field. Why would someone like a film director hire a musician to compose original music when they can simply enter in text prompts to generate something instead? Imagine someone using A.I. to have a spoken word poem created. Could these creations ever be as good and relevant as what a human would come up with? Without feelings, human experience, and intention to filter through, a machine is unable to create something truly authentic, relatable, and relative. That's what makes human creativity so powerful.

Award-winning science fiction author Ted Chiang says, "It is a fundamentally dehumanizing technology because it treats us as less than what we are: creators and apprehenders of meaning. It reduces the amount of intention in the world."

It is easy to see how companies promoting the use of A.I. could have ulterior motives. The good news is that as consumers we have a choice: if we disapprove of the lack of ethics of a company or their owner and dislike their products and services, we can stop supporting them. We can choose to live in a way that is best for our own creativity, productivity, and intellect. We still have plenty of time to re-think if and how we want to use A.I personally and in society as a whole.

So, should we stop marveling at the works of Mozart, Stephen Hawking, Ella Fitzgerald, Picasso, Mary Oliver, da Vinci, or so many others who have enhanced our lives using their natural intelligence? Does every endeavor we undertake need to be delivered instantaneously and without human contemplation?

Take your time to wonder, think, daydream, and create, and may human intelligence and creativity never be replaced by something artificial.

Extras

- **Images**
- **Lyrics to "Organic Intelligence"**
- **Reference Material**

Images

How we are being led to see
A.I. by the industry.

Images

Let's continue to see human intelligence as most important.

Images

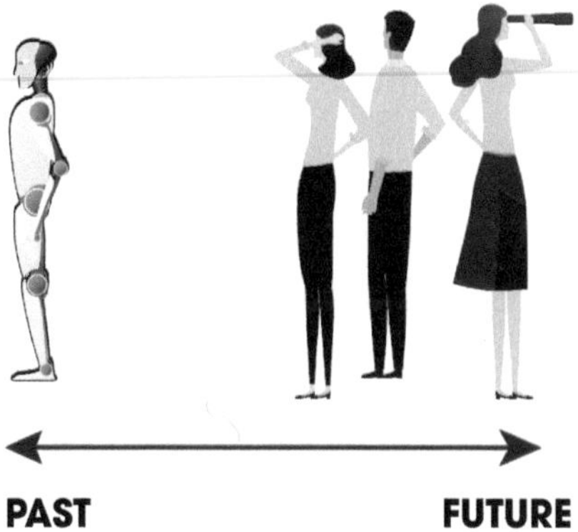

A.I. appears to use only input from the past to output variations and imitations. Humans can use the past <u>and</u> future to forge new ideas that stem from memories, dreams, hopes, and desires.

Lyrics to "Organic Intelligence"

Organic Intelligence

Song by Michael Faeth (2024)

good morning
had coffee with peace
Beethoven
to make it complete

drama later with
Shakespeare
an authentic voice
to hear

evening painted by
van Gogh
something you feel
and know

like
Prince, Cobain, Lennon, Hendrix
worth more than
some high tech trick

OI
OI

theory at night
on a beam
Einstein
didn't need your machine

OI

See the music video at:
youtube.com/@michaelfaeth

Reference Materials

Bicycle Diaries by David Byrne
Chapter "San Francisco." Paperback published by Penguin Publishing Group, 2009.

"Why A.I. Isn't Going to Make Art"
By Ted Chiang, *newyorker.com*, Aug. 2024.

"Yuval Noah Harari Warns AI Will Take Over Language, Law, and Power at WEF"
YouTube video from DRM News, 2026.

"Nvidia's Jensen Huang Makes Bold AI Predictions At Davos"
YouTube video from Forbes, 2026.